Managing ProjectLibre

An Introduction to Projects

David P Mork

Managing ProjectLibre

An Introduction to Projects

ISBN-13: 978-1511622202
ISBN-10: 1511622202

First Edition
April 2015

▪ MANAGING PROJECTLIBRE ▪

Contents

1.   Introduction to Projects

Project management is the process and activity of planning, organizing, motivating, and controlling resources, procedures and processes to achieve specific goals. A project is a temporary endeavor designed to produce a unique product, service or result with a defined beginning and end.

The project manager is the individual ultimately responsible for the project. This individual ensures the project scope is delivered within the allocated budget and within the planned schedule. A project is considered successful if the project deliverables meet quality expectations, the project spending stays within the limits of the project budget, and the project is completed by the target date established in the schedule.

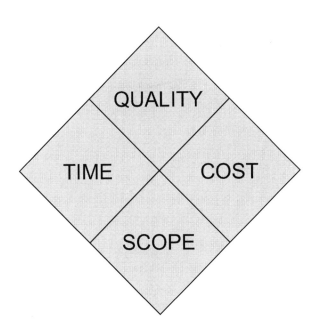

Individuals associated with a project are referred to as project stakeholders. Project stakeholders are any individual or group with a vested interest in the project outcomes. Stakeholders include the project manager, members of the project team, customers that will receive the results of the project, the project sponsor and the project champion who provides support to ensure resources are made available to the project team.

The project life cycle refers to a series of activities necessary to fulfill project goals or objectives. Projects vary in size and complexity, but, no matter how large or small, all projects can be mapped to the following life cycle structure.

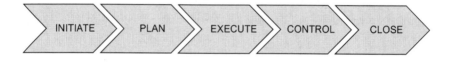

Initiation involves starting and defining the project as well as documenting the overview of the project and appointing the project team. Planning involves setting out the roadmap for the project by planning the project tasks, resources, budget, scope, constraints, deliverables and other similar items. Execution involves creating the project deliverables and executing the project plan. Even though some diagrams may include controlling as part of executing, it is ongoing throughout the life cycle. Closure involves winding-down the project by releasing staff, handing over deliverables to the customer and completing a post project review.

1.1   Initiating

The first phase of project management is the initiation phase. During the initiation phase the project is defined in terms of scope, the estimated schedule, and the planned budget. These three factors may change over time and require the project manager and project team to adapt to new or revised scope, budget cuts, or schedule accelerations. Projects can often fail if the scope changes too much and the goals cannot be met in the required time or budget.

The result of the initiation phase is a project charter. The project charter document outlines the work to be completed, defines the project budget and schedule, and identifies the key stakeholders, such as the project owner and project champion. This document becomes a type of contract for the project team by establishing the goals the team is expected to reach.

PROJECT CHARTER	
Project Name	
Project Sponsor	
Project Manager	
Team Members	
Stakeholders	
Date Chartered	
Start Date	
Target Completion	
Charter Statement	
Mission Statement	
Problem Statement	
Project Description	
Business Need	
Products/Services	

1.2   Planning

The second project management phase is based on the project charter established in the initiation phase. The planning phase is used to carry out a detailed analysis of the project as it was defined in the project charter and develop a plan to deliver the project.

During the planning phase the project scope is further investigated to provide a more detailed view of the expected deliverables and the corresponding costs and timelines. Once the scope is clearly defined and requirements identified, a more accurate budget and schedule can be established.

A work breakdown structure is commonly used to dissect a project into smaller components. This makes it easier to understand all of the activities that must take place to deliver the project. The work breakdown structure looks similar to an organizational chart where the project is broken down into deliverables or phases, activities needed to prepare the deliverable, and the individual tasks that must be executed to complete the project.

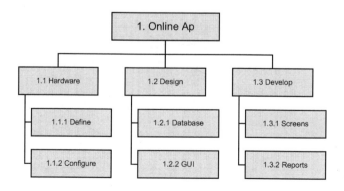

The bottom level tasks of the work breakdown structure are commonly referred to as work packages. These work packages are smaller units of work that can be assigned to team members. These work packages help distribute workload across the team and improve estimations and reporting. By estimating resources and time at the work package level, the project manager is able to provide more accurate estimates.

The work breakdown structure also helps to communicate the project execution by breaking down the project into smaller and more manageable pieces. This structure is used as input into another planning tool called the Gantt chart. The Gantt chart is a bar chart where horizontal bars represent lengths of times for scheduled activities. The chart often uses colors or shaded lines to show the project baseline and work that has been completed.

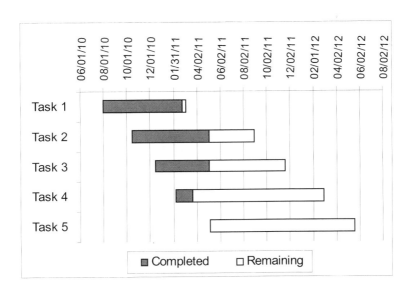

The Gantt chart also supports linked tasks to indicate the dependency of a task's start date or end date on the start or end date of another task. Using the Gantt chart, the project manager can outline all of the tasks that must be completed, identify the duration and schedule for each task, and determine the overall timelines for the project. By linking task dependencies the Gantt chart can be used to show the critical path in the project. This chart is also frequently used to track the performance of the project during the execution phase.

Once the tasks are identified from the work breakdown structure, a resource budget may be created. The resource budget is used to calculate the cost of the materials used and the time of the project members. In this budget calculation each task may be associated with one or more project team members or outside resources. Sometimes an expected estimate is calculated, however in some projects a three-point estimate that includes expected, low and high values for time and costs.

Resources are not always calculated for every project. For example, if you were writing a book you may only wish to create a project that included your expected tasks and the time to complete each task without tracking the cost of your own labor as a resource. For most projects, however, expenses should be identified and categorized in order to determine and justify the project's business case and estimate the financial budget.

1.3 Executing

Once the project scope, budget, and schedule plans are underway, the project can move to the execution phase where the project plans are carried out. This phase requires careful coordination and communication by the project manager and team members to ensure the plan is executed properly.

In the execution phase, the project manager guides the project team and coordinates all activities so that the plan is carried out according to schedule, budget and other constraints. The team must ensure the project deliverables meet the quality expectations of the customer.

One of the key activities for the project manager in the execution phase is communication. During the project execution phase the project manager must communicate with all project stakeholders. The stakeholders must stay engaged so that they are able to provide the needed support, respond to important project decisions, and are more likely to accept and adopt the project deliverables. To meet these goals a communications plan is often prepared.

A project communications plan is established to ensure the project manager and project team provides the type of communication needed for each project stakeholder. The plan should include clearly stated objectives, a stakeholder analysis, the communications strategy and potential issues and risks.

The Executing phase includes several other processes that enable the completion of the work defined in the project plan. During project execution, the project plans may change depending on the issue logs and change requests. Most of the project budget is used in this phase.

Directing and managing project work is a large part of execution. Some outputs of this process are deliverables, work performance data, and change requests. Some activities in this process include managing risks, performing activities to accomplish project objectives, and managing sellers and suppliers.

Quality must also be managed during execution. This process involves auditing of quality requirements and quality control measurements. The process essentially makes sure that the quality standards and operational definitions are being used during project execution.

1.4 Controlling

While the project execution phase is underway, the project manager must also monitor and control the project. During this phase the project manager watches over the project to ensure all hurdles are removed, decisions are made, and the path for delivery is cleared.

During this phase the project manager evaluates the progress and identifies issues that must be addressed, and potential risks that may prevent the project from reaching its goals. As the issues and risks are identified, the project team works together to respond to the issues or mitigate or remove the risks. This process enables the project team to be more proactive in dealing with uncertainty during the project rather than reacting to issues as they are encountered.

Most projects will encounter change. The scope defined at the beginning of the project is often incomplete or the business environment or requirements change. The project team must expect that changes to the project scope will occur. As these changes are introduced, a formalized process should be in place so that the project team can address any changes and also identify scope creep.

Scope creep in project management refers to uncontrolled changes or growth in a project's scope. This can occur when the scope of a project is not properly defined, documented or controlled and can cause a project to fail to meet time and cost constraints.

The project change management process should handle changes to the scope as they occur. The project manager should review potential changes along with estimates the change will have on the overall project budget and schedule. If the project owner determines the change is worth the investment, project manager executes a change order and documents and adjusts the project plan to accommodate the new scope.

CHANGE REQUEST		
Originator: _____	**Date:** _____	
Product: _____	**Change#:** _____	
Item: _____		
Reason: _____		
Priority: _____		
Description: _____		
Evaluation: _____		
Estimates: _____		
Approvals:		
[ ] Approved [ ] Denied [ ] On Hold		
Signature: _____	Date: _____	
Signature: _____	Date: _____	
Signature: _____	Date: _____	

If, however, the project owner decides the proposed change is not worth the investment or delay, then the change is rejected and the project team will continue to execute the existing plan without the requested change.

1.5 Closing

Projects are temporary and must end at some point. The final phase of the project management process is the closing phase. During the closing phase the project is concluded as the project owner approves the project deliverables. The project manager leads the team in a session where the lessons learned from the project are identified and documented. Any improvements to the project processes are determined and the processes are updated. The project manager may conduct an evaluation of the team members during this phase as well. At the end of the closing phase, all project artifacts are closed and archived for future reference. At this point, the project is considered complete and the project team members may be assigned to other work or other projects.

Even though there is a process for projects to follow, projects are not always successful. Project teams often are not able to deliver the project scope within the estimated budget and schedule. This should not be too surprising considering that projects are unique, complex, and require work of cross disciplinary specialists from across the organization.

Projects can fail for a number of different reasons. Sometimes projects do not have a champion in an organization or estimates are often not accurate. Other times the process is not followed and the team tries to take shortcuts. For these reasons effective software tools are essential to successful project management.

2.   ProjectLibre Basics

ProjectLibre, developed by Marc O'Brien and Laurent Chretienneau, is open source software that is an alternative to commercial software like Microsoft Project. It is free software and is compatible with several file types. The software includes task management, work breakdown structures, resource allocation and charts that provide a clear view of the critical path of the project.

ProjectLibre was developed by the founders the OpenProj software after that project was suspended. OpenProj was developed at Projity by Marc O'Brien, Howard Katz and Laurent Chretienneau in 2007. It moved out of beta with the release of Version 1.0, on January 10, 2008. Projity was later acquired by Serena Software in 2008. The founders announced that they forked the OpenProj software and released a new version called ProjectLibre in August 2012. ProjectLibre was voted as the open source Project of the Month for October, 2012 by the SourceForge community.

Compared to Microsoft Project, which it closely emulates, ProjectLibre has a similar user interface including a ribbon-style menu and a similar approach to construction of a project plan. The columns look the same as for Microsoft Project. Costing features are comparable and labor, hourly rate, material usage, and fixed costs are all provided. The ProjectLibre files are mostly compatible with Microsoft Project 2010, but ProjectLibre does not include the custom reporting options of that product.

2.1 Main Screen

The main screen of ProjectLibre is shown below. Note the main components of the dialog, which include the save and undo commands at the top, menu tabs below that, the ribbon toolbar directly below the menu, a spreadsheet view with the project tasks and a Gantt bar chart view that uses horizontal bars to represent the length of tasks. Each time you select a new menu tab item some or all of the commands groups in the ribbon toolbar will change. The optional views at the bottom of the screen can be changed using the view commands directly to the right of the menu tabs.

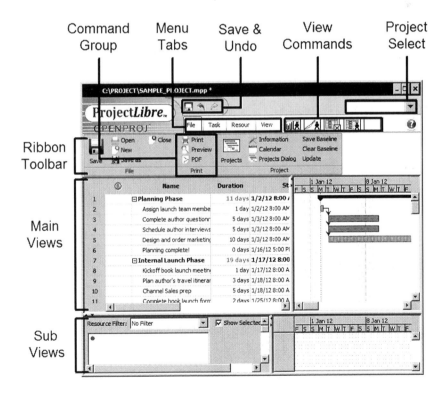

Above the menu are the Save, Undo and Redo buttons. To the right of the menu are five icons used to display options charts that show histograms, task usage and resource usage. The blank icon on the far right will hide the display of the optional charts. The drop box above the chart allows you to quickly switch projects.

The question mark or help icon to the right of the chart icons will display the help dialog. The ProjectLibre license is the Common Public Attribution License (CPAL) which is a free software license approved by the Open Source Initiative in 2007. The "Go to online help" button may display a website page with an error. Some users have posted a "ProjectLibre Manual" that can be found on docs.google.com. Finally, as shown in the help dialog below, ProjectLibre Version 1.5.9 for Microsoft Windows was used for all the screens and demonstrations in this book.

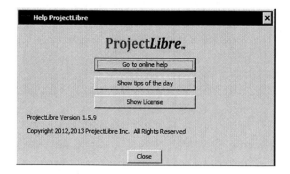

2.2   File Menu Tab

The File menu tab will cause the File, Print and Project toolbars to be displayed. The File toolbar group has the standard commands you may be used to including Open, New, Save, Save as and close.

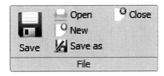

Note that each time you start the ProjectLibre software it will display the Welcome dialog with options to Create Project or Open Project. These buttons perform the same functions as the New and Open buttons on the File toolbar.

The Save dialog allows you to save projects as a ProjectLibre file (*.pod) or as a Microsoft Project (*.xml) file. Note that version 1.5.9 of ProjectLibre is designed to be compatible with Microsoft Project 2010.

The Open dialog allows you to open projects that have been saved as a ProjectLibre file (*.pod), or a native Microsoft Project 2010 (*.mpp) file, or a Microsoft Project XML file or as a Gnome Planner file type. If you try to open MPP files that have been saved with newer versions of Microsoft Project the ProjectLibre software may crash or temporarily stop working and you may need to terminate the process or restart your computer.

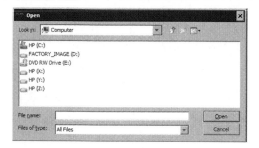

- ProjectLibre (*.pod)
- Microsoft Project (*.mpp)
- Microsoft Project (*.xml)
- Gnome Planner (*.planner)

The Print toolbar provides commands to Preview and Print the task spreadsheet and bar chart or create a PDF file. The Report button associated with the View menu tab has additional printing options.

The Project toolbar group below the File menu displays buttons for Projects, Information, Calendar, Projects Dialog, Save Baseline, Clear Baseline and Update.

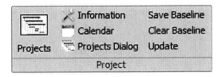

The Projects button will display a list of active projects in a table format with a number of columns that summarize critical information.

Name	Start	Finish	Manager	Status Date
PROJECT 1	7/9/12 8:00 AM	11/29/12 5:00 PM	BOB	3/27/15 5:00 PM
PROJECT 2	3/27/15 8:00 AM	3/27/15 8:00 AM	DAVID	3/27/15 5:00 PM

The Information button shows the project information for the current project that is selected in the dropdown list in the upper right of the screen.

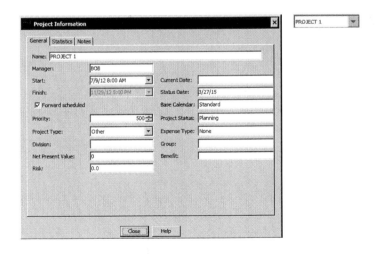

The Calendar button allows the user to change the working calendar and the Options... button in that screen allows the Duration Settings, such as hours in a day, to be changed.

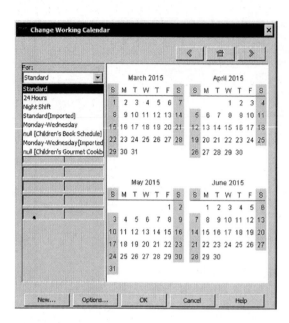

The Projects Dialog shows the same list as the Projects button, but opens a new dialog that does not affect the task spreadsheet or the bar chart.

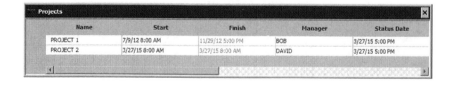

Save Baseline and Clear Baseline allow the user to save or clear up to ten project baselines.

When the actual schedule starts deviating from the planned schedule it is a good time to create a baseline. In the example below you can see that painting took longer than expected and the project ended after the original baseline.

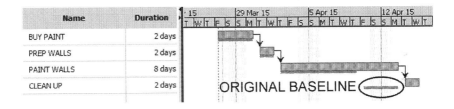

Clicking on Clear Baseline will display the baseline dialog and allow you to clear individual baselines. Use the dropdown list to select the baseline that you wish to clear and click OK to clear the data.

The Update button will display the Update Project dialog box shown below. This screen will let you automatically change the Percent Complete of tasks that are scheduled.

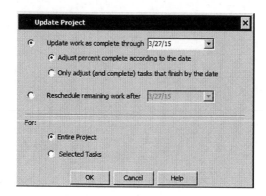

In the example below the black lines in the bar chart show the completion of individual tasks. The check next to each task number shows the task is done.

Selected Tasks can be updated by holding the Ctrl button and clicking on task numbers before you click the Update button.

2.3   Task Menu Tab

The Task menu will cause the Views, Clipboard and Task toolbars to be displayed. The Views command group allow you to quickly change the spreadsheet and Gantt chart to a Network diagram, a Work Breakdown Structure (WBS) or a view of Task Usage.

An example Network diagram is shown below. A network diagram is a flow chart that includes all of the project elements and how they relate to one another. It is widely used because it is easy to read and not only depicts the sequence of activities in the project, but also shows parallel activities and the links between each activity.

The Work Breakdown Structure (WBS) is shown below. It is a hierarchical chart with nodes that represent all the tasks in a project. A Work Breakdown Structure is a very valuable and important project management tool used for project planning.

The Task Usage view is shown below. It shows hourly work based on information entered. The left half of the view summarizes the total allocation of hours to each task while the right half (the schedule plan) shows the hourly profile of available hours against chronological time.

	Name	Work	Duration		24	27	30	Apr 2015 02	05	08	11
1	BUY PAINT	16 hours	2 days	Work			8h	8h			
2	PREP WALLS	16 hours	2 days	Work				16h			
3	PAINT WALLS	64 hours	8 days	Work					16h	16h	24h	8h

The Task toolbar group is shown below. It contains buttons to Insert or Delete tasks, to Indent and Outdent them and to Link or Unlink them. It also includes buttons for task Information, Calendar, Notes, Resources, Baselines and Update. Note that many of these functions may also be performed by either right clicking on a task or by double clicking on a task.

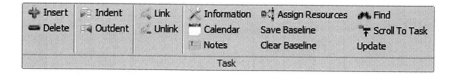

The Insert and Delete buttons work similar to the same functions found on most spreadsheets. You may click on a task number to highlight the task, and then click the Insert button to add a new task above the selected task for click the Delete button to delete that task.

The Indent and Outdent buttons are used to group subtasks. The Indent button creates a group of subtasks under the task above them. The Outdent is the inverse of the Indent command and simply removes a level from the hierarchy. In the example below, there are four subtasks below the third task PAINT WALLS.

	ℹ	Name	Duration			
1		BUY PAINT	1 day			
2		PREP WALLS	2 days			
3		PAINT WALLS	8 days			
4		KITCHEN	2 days			
5		BATHROOM	2 days			
6		LIVINGROOM	2 days			
7		BEDROOM	2 days			

After the Predecessors are assigned, the tasks have been selected and indented to show they are all subtasks of PAINT WALLS. Note that the red bar for PAINT WALLS has now become a solid black bar that is above the subtasks. The small box with the "-" symbol can be used to collapse the subtasks and condense the spreadsheet and report. To expand the subtasks again simply click on the "+" button to the left of PAINT WALLS.

The Link and Unlink commands connect tasks and subtasks when the elements dependent on one another. To use the commands on the Task ribbon, first select the link to be operated upon in the spreadsheet by clicking on one of the two task rows connected by the link to be modified. Then hold down the Ctrl key and click again to highlight a second row. Finally, click the Link or Unlink command from the toolbar.

Another way to link and unlink tasks is to enter the task number in the Predecessors column of the spreadsheet. In the example below, the BATHROOM, LIVINGROOM and BEDROOM have all been changed to show that the KITCHEN must be painted first by entering the KITCHEN task number as a predecessor.

Note that be default subtasks are linked to the summary task. You cannot enter the summary task as a predecessor to a subtask or the software will display an error.

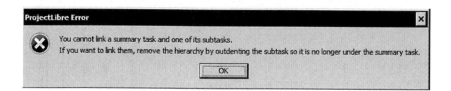

2.4   Resource Menu Tab

The Resource menu tab will display command groups for resource views and resource commands. The Views group provides commands that allow you to change the main views to a Resource Breakdown Structure (RBS) spreadsheet view. The Resource command group displays commands that allow you to change information about individual resources or group resources together.

An example resource spreadsheet is shown below. Information can be entered directly into the spreadsheet, or you can double click on a resource line to access a dialog with the details for that resource. Another method to accomplish the same result is to click on time on a resource and then click on the Information command button to display the resource dialog box.

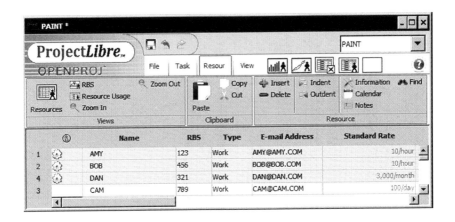

The Standard Rate can be in minutes, hours, week, months or years. Below are some of the abbreviations that can be used for these rates. For example, to enter ten dollars per hour you can just enter "10/h" to save time.

- /m   /minute
- /h   /hour
- /w   /week
- /mo   /month
- /y   /year

The General tab for Resource Information is shown below. The "RBS" field can be used to store resource identification like an employee or vendor number. The Type of resource can be Work or Material. If the Type is Material the rate will show as a cost per unit of Material Label. For example, if AMY charges $1,000 to paint a hour the Type should be changed to Material and the Material Label should be changed to HOUSE. The Base Calendar may be Standard, 24 Hours or Night Shift.

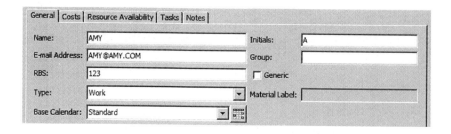

An example RBS view is shown below. The costs have been calculated based on the standard rate of each resource and which tasks they have been assigned in the project.

AMY			BOB			DAN	
Cost	$80.00		Cost	$160.00		Cost	$300.00
Budget	$0.00		Budget	$0.00		Budget	$0.00

The Resource Usage view is shown below. It displays the tasks assigned to each resource and the scheduled dates to complete the tasks.

	Name	Work			29 Mar 15						
					5	M	T	W	T	F	S
1	AMY	8 hours	Work		0h	8h	0h	0h	0h	0h	0h
	BUY PAINT	8 hours	Work			8h					
2	BOB	16 hours	Work		0h	0h	8h	8h	0h	0h	0h
	PREP WALLS	16 hours	Work				8h	8h			
4	DAN	16 hours	Work		0h	0h	0h	0h	8h	8h	0h
	PAINT WALLS	16 hours	Work						8h	8h	
3	CAM	0 hours	Work		0h	0h	0h	0h	0h	0h	0h

The Resource command group is shown below. The Indent and Outdent functions are powerful in making changes to the hierarchical structure of the RBS, similar to the Indent and Outdent functions discussed in the Task command. The Information and Notes commands display the Resource Information dialog for the selected resource. The Calendar command allows you to change the working calendar.

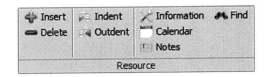

2.5 Views Menu Tab

The Views menu tab displays the Task Views and Resource Views command groups discussed above. In addition to these command groups, the Other Views, Sub-views and Filters command groups are also shown.

The Other views command group, shown below, allows you to change the main view to Projects or Report. The Projects view shows the current list of projects that are loaded in the dropdown box at the top of the screen that is used to quickly switch projects.

The project spreadsheet is shown below. If you double click on one of the project lines, the Project Information dialog will be shown. You can also enter information directly into the spreadsheet.

Name	Start	Finish	Manager	Status Date
PAINT	3/30/15 8:00 AM	4/3/15 5:00 PM	DAVID	3/27/15 5:00 PM
SAMPLE	1/2/12 8:00 AM	2/29/12 5:00 PM	MARY	3/27/15 5:00 PM

If you click on the Report button the main view will change to the report view. The available reports are Resource Information, Project Details, Task Information and Who Does What.

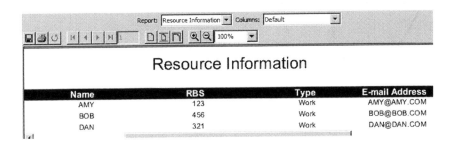

For some of the report views a Columns dropdown box will appear with options to change the columns in the report, as shown below.

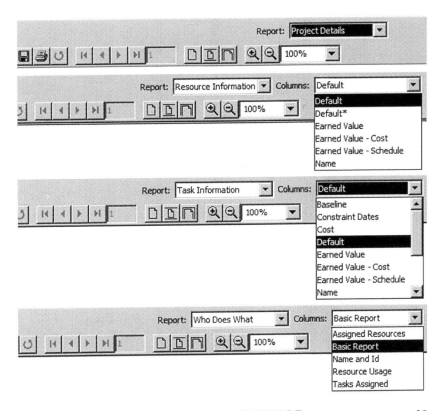

The Sub-views command group has commands that display the optional views at the bottom of the screen. These views include Histogram, Charts, Task Usage and Resource Usage. The No sub window command will close the optional report view. Note that these commands are identical to the command buttons at the top of the screen to the right of the tab menu bar.

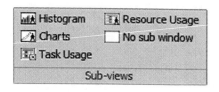 

The Filters command group includes three functions that allow you to Filter, Sort or Group the Tasks or Resources to those you want to view on your screen. These functions also influence the content of the reports.

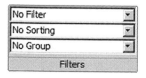

Note that the Filter options are not identical for Task Views and Resource Views and the selections will change as you switch views.

Task Views   Resource Views

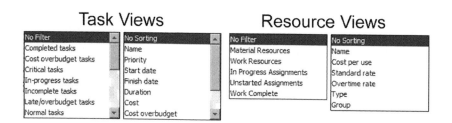

3.   Starting a Project

Project management is the application of knowledge, skills, tools and techniques to manage a temporary endeavor undertaken to create a product or service. It requires the knowledge of the project life cycle and it an understanding of the human elements in the project team. The project life cycle can be divided into four phases: define, plan, execute and close.

You can start a new project by defining its objectives, scope, purpose and deliverables to be produced. Many of the items shown below are kept in the project documentation or project charter.

- Business Case for Project
- Project Goals and Objectives
- Scope of the Project
- Critical Project Deliverables
- List of Customers and Stakeholders
- List of Project Team Members
- Key Roles and Responsibilities
- Project Organizational Structure
- Implementation Plan
- Assumptions, Risks and Constraints

Once you have a document that defines the project you can start the planning phase. To plan the project you will need to work with tasks, resources and costs. These are three of the most important terms used in project management software. They are the core elements to be manipulated and organized in the program.

- Tasks
- Resources
- Costs

Tasks are the fundamental building blocks for a project schedule. Each task represents a unit of work, a step toward completing a project. Tasks often need to take a hierarchical form to break a complex project down into manageable chunks.

Resources are required to carry out the project tasks. They can be people, equipment, facilities, funding, or anything else required for the completion of a project activity. Resources are shared entities. All the people and materials owned by your organization are shared by all projects supported by the organization.

Costs refer to the monetary value or financial pricing of a specific project activity. Costs are usually assigned to people resources with hourly, weekly or monthly rates. Costs can also represent the amount of money paid to acquire materials.

3.1   New Project

Start the ProjectLibre software and select Create Project at the welcome screen. You may also click on the New command in the file tab to open the New Project dialog box.

In the New Project dialog box enter WRITE BOOK for the Project Name and enter your name as Manager. For the Start Date enter 1/9/2017 and select the check mark for a Forward schedule.

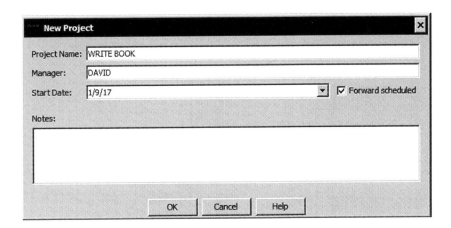

3.2   Project Information

Click on the Information command button in the Project command group to display the Project Information dialog box. The General and Statistics tabs contain a summary of the project information and additional information can be saved in the Notes tab.

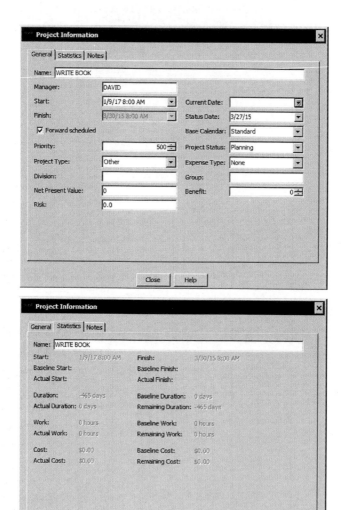

3.3 Working Calendar

The Calendar is the primary means by which you control when each task and resource is schedule for work. Click on the Calendar command button to display the project calendar. ProjectLibre includes multiple base calendars that serve as the calendar for a plan. The Standard calendar has working hours from 8 A.M. to 5 P.M with a one-hour break each Monday through Friday. The 24 Hour calendar has no nonworking time and the Night Shift calendar is from 11 P.M. to 8 A.M.

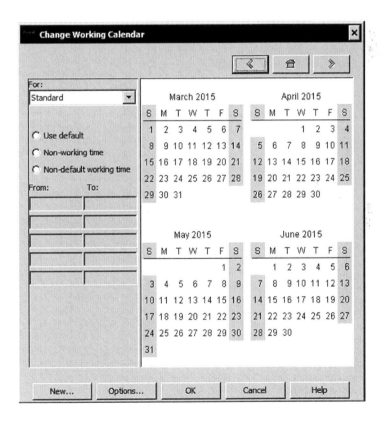

To create a new calendar click on the New... button at the bottom of the screen. For example, perhaps the hours in your organization are 9 A.M. to 6 P.M. so you want to create a new calendar for those hours. Simply click on the new button and Create a new Base Calendar called NINETOSIX as shown below and click the OK button.

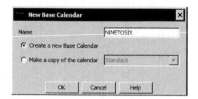

Next, click on the "M" in the calendar and change the time to Non-default working time and change 8:00 to 9:00 and 17:00 to 18:00. Do this for each working day and then click OK to save the changes.

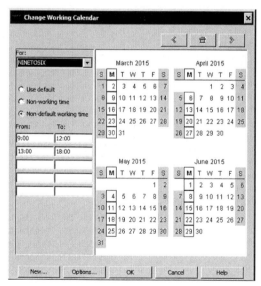

Finally, you will need to open the Project Information dialog box and change the Base Calendar from Standard to your new calendar that you named NINETOSIX.

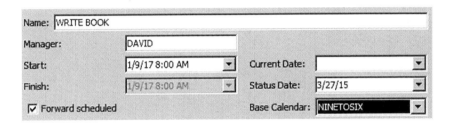

You may also click on individual days in the calendar and set them as non-working time. For example, if January 23 is a holiday in your organization, click on that date then select Non-working time and click OK to save.

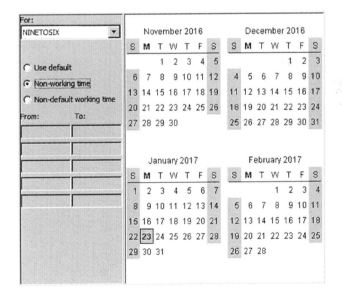

4. Creating Tasks

Tasks are the basic building blocks of a project. They represent the work that needs to be done to accomplish the goals of the project. The main components of each task are duration, dependencies and resource requirements. Tasks may be summary tasks, subtasks or milestones.

In the spreadsheet view click directly below the Name column and enter the following tasks.

- 1. DESIGN COVER
- 2. CREATE OUTLINE
- 3. WRITE BOOK
- 4. EDIT PROOF
- 5. SUBMIT FINAL

Your spreadsheet view should look like the screen below.

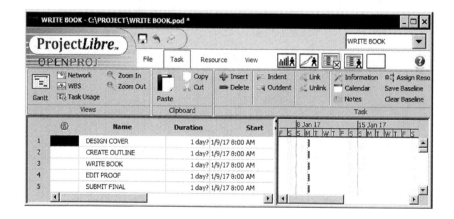

4.1 Setting Task Durations

Each task may take a certain amount of time. The duration of a task represents how long you expect it will take to complete the task. Durations can be in minutes, hours, days, weeks or months. For small projects you may want to use hours and larger projects often use days to estimate the duration of tasks. When entering task durations you may use abbreviations to set the unit of time. For example, entering "1w" will be recorded as five days or one week.

- 1m   1 minute
- 1h   1 hour
- 1d   1 day
- 1w   1 week
- 1mo   1 month
- 1y   1 year

Edit the Duration of each of the tasks in your project so they are all one day, except set WRITE BOOK to five days as shown below.

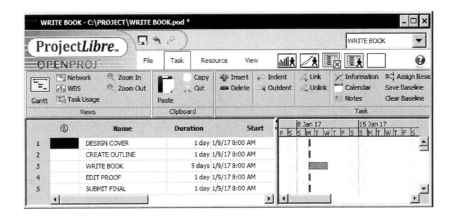

4.2   Setting Milestones

Milestones are significant events that are reached in the project plan. They are special tasks with no duration. Milestones are typically used to mark major outcome like the completion of a deliverable.

In the spreadsheet view double click on the SUBMIT FINAL task to open the Task Information dialog. Click on the Advanced tab and select Display task as milestone to create a milestone.

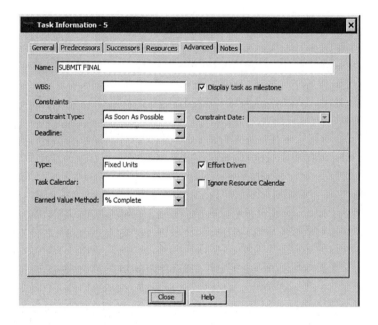

The task should now show a black diamond to represent the milestone.

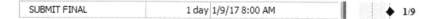

| SUBMIT FINAL | 1 day | 1/9/17 8:00 AM | ♦ 1/9 |

4.3   Creating Summary Tasks

A summary task summarizes another set of tasks. Normally, the summary task is not assigned a resource. This is because the summary task's start and completion dates are derived from the earliest subtask's start date and latest subtask's finish date. As each task is completed, the summary task's overall completion is updated as well. Normally, a summary task is not linked to other tasks. Using summary tasks makes reading a Work Breakdown Structure (WBS) easier because they can use a logical grouping.

In the WRITE BOOK project use the Insert command to add CHAPTER 1, CHAPTER 2 and CHAPTER 3 below the WRITE BOOK task. Next, hold the Ctrl key down and click on each of the new tasks. Finally, click on the Indent command button to define these three tasks as subtasks below the summary task WRITE BOOK. When you have finished your project should look like the screen below.

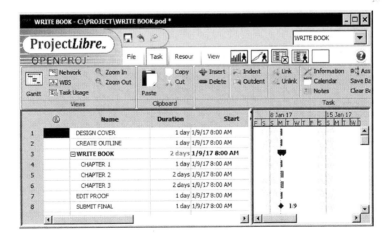

4.4 Entering Task Dependencies

You may have noticed that the WRITE BOOK task, which originally had duration of five days, now has duration of two days. This is because the tasks do not have any dependencies so the software assumes they can all be completed at the same time. To add dependencies enter the following information in the Predecessors column of the view spreadsheet.

- DESIGN COVER
- CREATE OUTLINE.........................1
- WRITE BOOK...............................2
- CHAPTER 1
- CHAPTER 2..............................4
- CHAPTER 3..............................5
- EDIT PROOF................................3
- SUBMIT FINAL..............................7

Your project Gantt chart should now look like the screen below. Note that the WRITE BOOK task again has duration of five days.

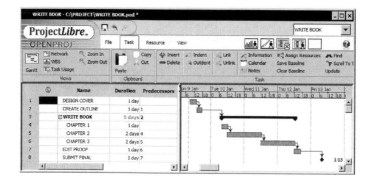

4.5   Linking Task Dependencies

The Link and Unlink command buttons can be used as an alternative to entering the Predecessor information. In the example below the first and second tasks have been selected using the Ctrl key and the mouse button. When the Link command button is clicked the Predecessor information is automatically filled in.

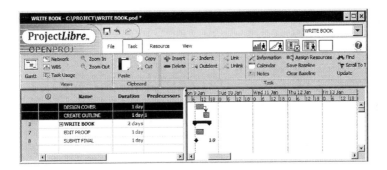

The same process can be used for each task by linking two tasks each time. The default type of dependency when linking tasks is FINISH TO START. That means that the first task must finish before the next task can begin.

Note that it is possible to also link tasks by dragging in the bar chart. Use the mouse to drag one task to connect it to another to link them. A line and a small link icon will appear as you drag each task.

4.6   Task Dependency Types

The default type of dependency when linking tasks is FINISH TO START. That can be changed in the Task Information dialog. To change the dependency type select a task in the spreadsheet then click on the Information command button. Select the Successors tab and click on the Type column. The following choices are available.

- FF   Finish to Finish

- FS   Finish to Start

- SF   Start to Finish

- SS   Start to Start

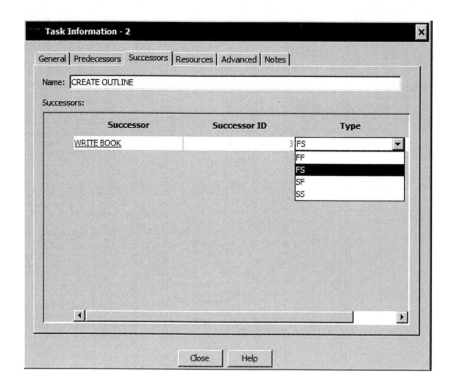

4.7 Using WBS Codes

Each task has a task number that is shown on the left side of the spreadsheet. However, you may want to use your own code in the "WBS" field instead. The WBS codes are often used similar to the numeric outline structure used in this book. For example, the section "4.7 Using WBS Codes" is a subsection of "4. Creating Tasks" in this chapter.

One method to change the WBS code is to click on the Advanced tab in the Task Information dialog box. The WBS code is below the name to the left of the "milestone" selection.

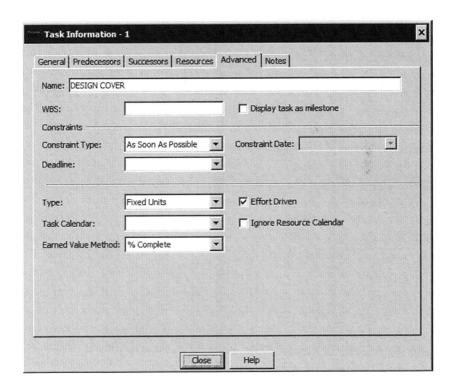

Another method that may be faster is to add the WBS code as a column in the task spreadsheet. To add a column to the spreadsheet, use the mouse to right-click on the column headers and select the "Insert Column..." menu command. Fine the "WBS" field and click OK to add the column.

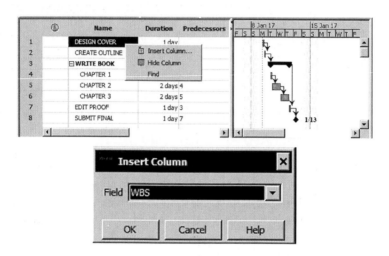

Note that you can use the mouse to drag the column header left or right and it will move between columns. Also, if you hold the mouse between columns until it changes to a sizing cursor you can resize the column.

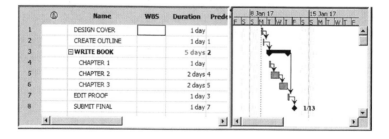

In the WRITE BOOK project below the WBS codes have been added to show major tasks and subtasks using an outline numbering method.

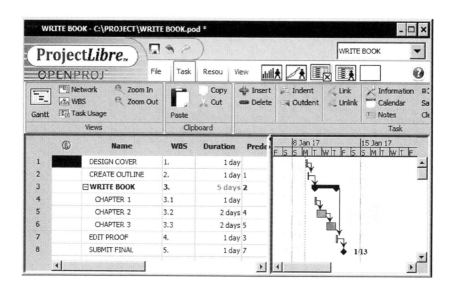

Once the WBS column has been added to the task spreadsheet it will be printed in the Task Information report when the Columns selection is changed to the project name. The "Hide Column..." can be used to remove columns from the spreadsheet and report.

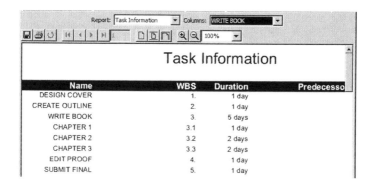

4.8   Task Splitting

Tasks normally continue uninterrupted until the task is complete. If you know that there will be interruptions or periods of inactivity on a task or if there are resource conflicts, you may need to split a task into two or more segments. To split a task use the mouse to right-click on the task bar in the Gantt view and select Split from the menu.

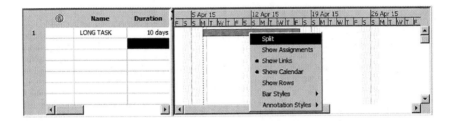

A special splitting cursor should appear as shown below.

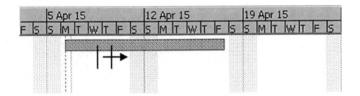

Use the mouse to left-click on the task bar where you want to split it. Note that a task may be split more than once.

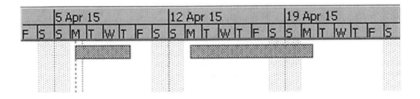

4.9 Total Project Duration

After you have entered all the task durations and dependencies you may want to know the total project duration. To find this information click on the File menu tab and in the Projects command group click on the Information command button. This will display the Project Information dialog box. Click on the Statistics tab and the project start, finish and duration will be displayed.

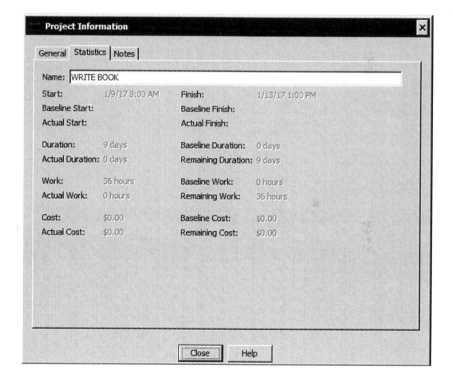

5. Creating Resources

Resources are people, equipment, material and other costs needed to perform the tasks in a project. Work resources are people and machines that need time to complete a task and have a cost associated with a unit of time. Material resources are consumables like bricks, wood or paint and are used independent of time.

Start a new project and select the Resource menu tab. Then select the Resources view to change your spreadsheet to show resources. Enter the work resources shown below.

- AMY $30 / hour
- BOB $30 / hour
- CAM $30 / hour
- DAN $30 / hour

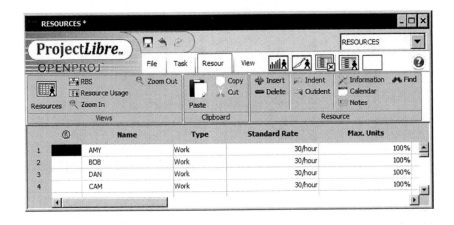

5.1 Creating Work Resources

Work resources may be the name of a person or they could represent a function like ACCOUNTANT, PAINTER, PLUMBER or even something like CONSULTANT. If you double click on the resource the Resource Information dialog will appear. Note that the software will automatically fill in Initials. You may want to use the RBS field for an identification number like employee or vendor number.

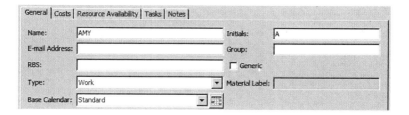

The Costs tab shows the Cost rate tables. Also the Accrue At dropdown box may be set to Start, End or Prorated. This tells the software when to charge the costs to the project. For example, a contractor may not bill the project until after all the work is complete.

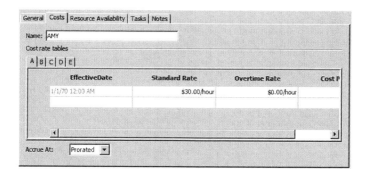

5.2   Creating Material Resources

Material resources are consumable items like wood, paper or paint. Enter PAINT as a new resource and change the Type to Material and the cost to $40 as shown below.

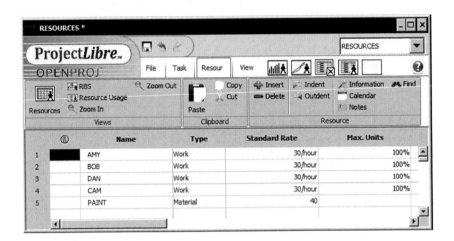

Double click on the PAINT resource and change the Material Label to GALLON and click Close to accept the change.

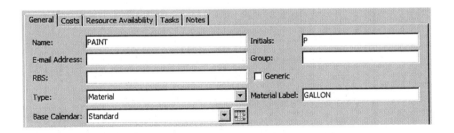

PAINT should now show 40 GALLON in the Resource spreadsheet. Save your project as PAINT HOUSE.

5	PAINT	Material	40 GALLON

6. Assigning Resources

Work and material resources must be assigned to tasks for costs to allocate in the project. Below is an estimate for the PAINT HOUSE project that was done with a spreadsheet program. In this chapter we will learn how to create those tasks and assign the work and material resources to the project.

	DAYS	LABOR	PAINT	TOTAL
PREP	1	$240		$240
OUTSIDE	2	$480	$160	$640
MAIN	1	$240	$80	$320
KITCHEN	1	$240	$80	$320
BATHROOMS	1	$240	$80	$320
BEDROOMS	1	$240	$80	$320
CLEAN	1	$240		$240
T O T A L S		**$1,920**	**$480**	**$2,400**

In the Task view enter the tasks in the PAINT HOUSE project and link them by entering the Predecessors information.

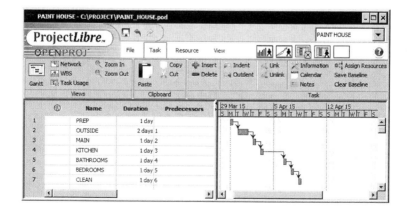

6.1 Assigning Work Resources

Double click on the PREP task to open the Task Information dialog. In the Resources tab there is a button on the right that can be used to assign resources.

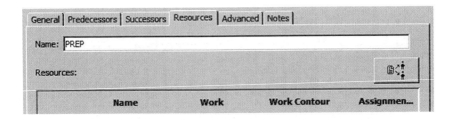

When you click on the button the Assign Resources dialog will be shown. You should see all the resources in your project here. Note that you can also access this screen directly by highlighting a task or several tasks and then clicking on the Assign Resources button in the Task command group.

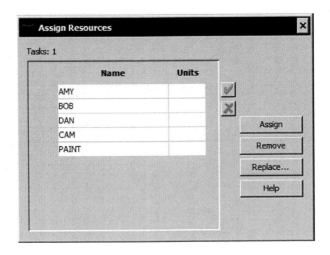

Click on AMY to highlight that resource then click on the Assign button. The Remove button can be used to remove the assignment.

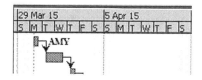

Name	Units
AMY	100%
BOB	
DAN	
CAM	
PAINT	

The main Gantt view should now show that AMY is assigned to the first task.

Repeat this process and assign a work resource for each task in the project. When you are done your Gantt chart should look similar to the screen below.

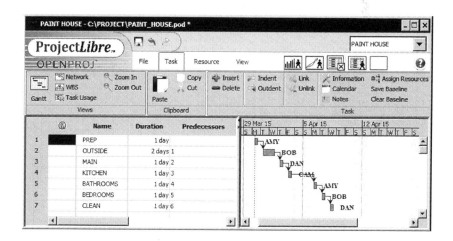

6.2 Assigning Material Resources

Material resources are assigned using the same method. Double click on the OUTSIDE task and assign 4 GALLONS of paint to that task.

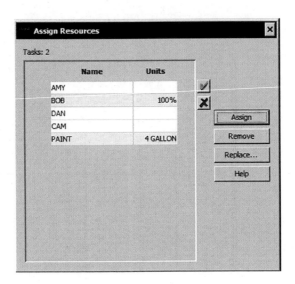

Open each painting task and assign the PAINT resource as shown below.

- OUTSIDE   4 GALLON
- MAIN   2 GALLON
- KITCHEN   2 GALLON
- BATHROOMS   2 GALLON
- BEDROOMS   2 GALLON

After you have assigned the PAINT resource to each painting task your Gantt chart should look similar to the screen below.

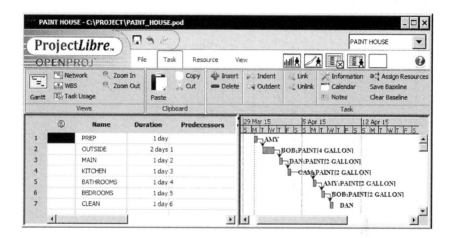

If you have entered all the information correctly your Project Information dialog box should show work of 64 hours and a project cost of $2,400.

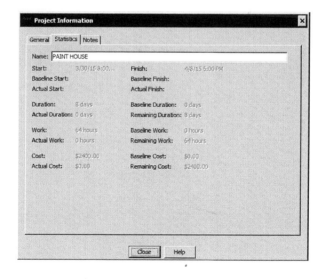

6.3 Overbooked Resources

Sometimes resources become overbooked. In the example below the project manager has accidentally scheduled DAN to perform PAINT INTERIOR and PAINT EXTERIOR at the same time.

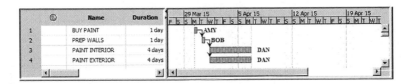

This conflict can be seen below in the Resource Usage view by looking at the total hours DAN is scheduled to work each day.

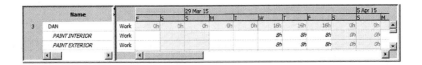

The over allocation can also be seen below in the Histogram sub-view by selecting DAN on the left. The black line in the histogram shows the total time that DAN is available to work. If you have a more complicated project it may be useful to change the Resource Filter to Work Resources, In Progress Assignments or Unstarted Assignments. Sub-views are explained in more detail in the next section.

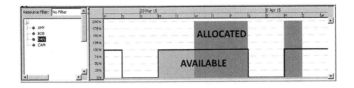

7. Sub Views

The Sub-views command group has commands that display the optional views at the bottom of the screen. These views include Histogram, Charts, Task Usage and Resource Usage. The No sub window command will close the optional report view.

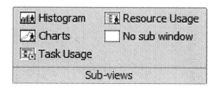

Clicking the Histogram icon will show the sub view for Histograms. The task or resource selected in the main view will be the source for data shown in the Histogram. In the example below the OUTSIDE task is selected and the sub view shows the usage. The blue bars show the selected resource, the green bar for the project and the black lines show the total availability.

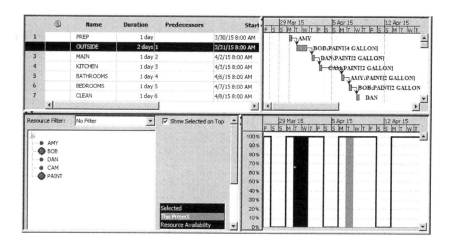

The second sub view icon is for charts. The chart sub view can be displayed as a cumulative line or as a histogram and can plot either work or cost. Note that you can use the Ctrl key to select more than one task in the main view. The screen below shows a cost histogram when all tasks have been selected.

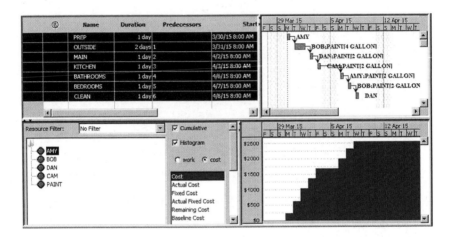

The screen below shows the cumulative work histogram for the first three tasks in the project.

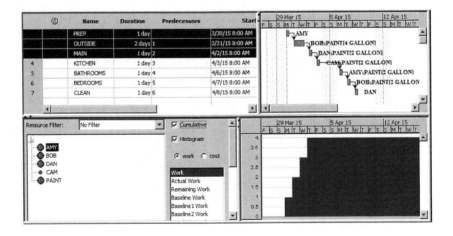

The third sub view icon is for task usage. The sub views in the screen below show the task usage for the OUTSIDE and MAIN tasks.

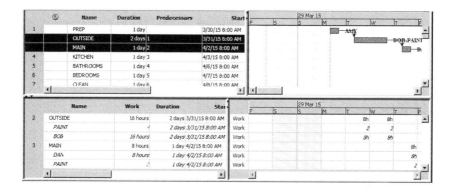

The final sub view icon is for resource usage. The screen below shows the resource usage sub views for the OUTSIDE and MAIN tasks.

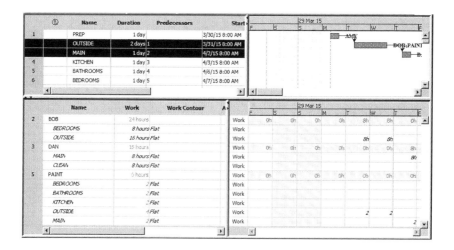

8. Reports

After you have created your project plan you may want to share some of the information with stakeholders and team members. There are several reports available for that purpose. This chapter will discuss the most useful reports at the start of the project.

The structure of the reporting system is shown below. The four types of reports are Project Details, Resource Information, Task Information and Who Does What.

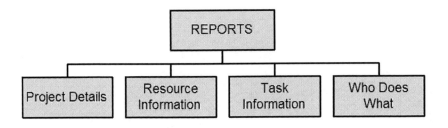

In addition to the Reports function, the Print and Print Preview commands can be used to print copies of the Gantt View, Network View, WBS View and RBS view. Unfortunately, the customization options for printing these views are limited.

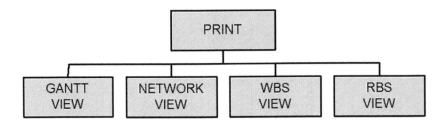

Below is the Project Details report. It provides much of the same information that is in the Project Information dialog.

PAINT HOUSE

Dates

Start	3/30/15 8:00 AM	Finish	4/8/15 5:00 PM
Baseline Start		Baseline Finish	
Actual Start		Actual Finish	

Duration

Scheduled	8 days	Remaining	8 days
Baseline	0 days	Actual	0 days
		Percent Complete	0%

Work

Scheduled	64 hours	Remaining	64 hours
Baseline	0 hours	Actual	0 hours

Costs

Scheduled	$2400.00	Remaining	$2400.00
Baseline	$0.00	Actual	$0.00
		Variance	$0.00

Notes

The example below is the Who Does What report. It lists what tasks are assigned to each resource.

Resource ID	Resource						
1	AMY						
Task ID	Task	Work	Assignment Units	Assignment		Start	Finish
1	PREP	8 hours		100%	0 days	3/30/15 8:00 AM	3/30/15 5:00 PM
5	BATHROOMS	8 hours		100%	0 days	4/6/15 8:00 AM	4/8/15 5:00 PM
		16 hours					
2	BOB						
Task ID	Task	Work	Assignment Units	Assignment		Start	Finish
2	OUTSIDE	16 hours		100%	0 days	3/31/15 8:00 AM	4/1/15 5:00 PM
6	BEDROOMS	8 hours		100%	0 days	4/7/15 8:00 AM	4/7/15 5:00 PM
		24 hours					
3	DAN						
Task ID	Task	Work	Assignment Units	Assignment		Start	Finish
3	MAIN	8 hours		100%	0 days	4/2/15 8:00 AM	4/2/15 5:00 PM
7	CLEAN	8 hours		100%	0 days	4/8/15 8:00 AM	4/8/15 5:00 PM
		16 hours					
4	CAM						
Task ID	Task	Work	Assignment Units	Assignment		Start	Finish
4	KITCHEN	8 hours		100%	0 days	4/3/15 8:00 AM	4/3/15 5:00 PM
		8 hours					

The Task Information with the Columns set to Cost is shown below. This report provides a summary of the cost of each task.

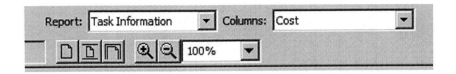

Task Information

ID	Name	Cost	Actual Cost	Remaining Cost
1	PREP	$ 240.00	$ 0.00	$ 240.00
2	OUTSIDE	$ 640.00	$ 0.00	$ 640.00
3	MAIN	$ 320.00	$ 0.00	$ 320.00
4	KITCHEN	$ 320.00	$ 0.00	$ 320.00
5	BATHROOMS	$ 320.00	$ 0.00	$ 320.00
6	BEDROOMS	$ 320.00	$ 0.00	$ 320.00
7	CLEAN	$ 240.00	$ 0.00	$ 240.00

The Print Preview for the WBS view is shown below. By adjusting the Scale to width percentage the report can be formatted to print on one page.

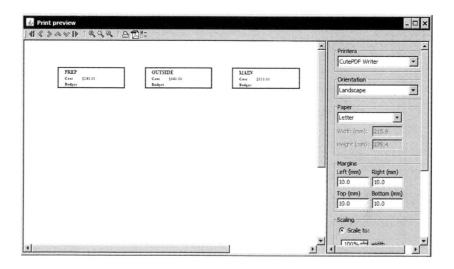

The example below shows the result of the report printed at 75%.

Note that the tasks can be moved on the screen with the mouse as shown below, but the Print commands restore the default positions.

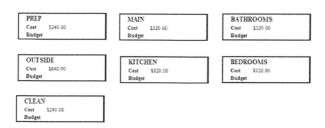

9.   Critical Path

The Critical Path Method (CPM) is a process of using a time path to reveal which activities are considered critical to the project. It is the sequence of schedule activities that determines the duration of the project. Project managers can also apply the critical path methodology technique to determine the amount of float on various logical network paths in the project schedule network to determine the minimum total project duration.

Another way of saying this is that the critical path is simply all the tasks that determine the end date in the project schedule. If one of those tasks is late by one day, then the project end date will be extended by one day. Tasks that are not on the critical path may sometimes be delayed without affecting the completion date of the project, but if a task on the critical path is delayed then the project will also be delayed.

Critical tasks are shown in red in ProjectLibre and tasks that are not critical are shown in blue. You can examine the Gantt chart and quickly identify the tasks that have some float compared to the tasks that have no slack.

Slack is the amount of time a task can be delayed without impacting the start date of a subsequent task. The critical path methodology is simply a technique to identify all the tasks that will directly impact the project end date.

In the example below OUTSIDE not linked to painting the INSIDE of the house. To finish the entire PAINTING project, the OUTSIDE task has some slack because it does not affect the timeline of the INSIDE summary task. It is shown in blue in the Gantt chart to reflect that it is not part of the critical path.

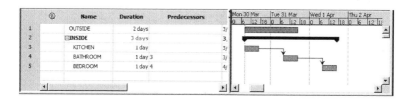

Now assume that for some reason the OUTSIDE task cannot start when the INSIDE task starts and the starting date is pushed out a few days. Now the OUTSIDE task becomes the critical path of the project and will turn red in the Gantt chart.

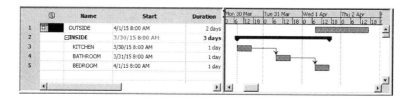

If the OUTSIDE painting task is moved back so it will complete at the same time as all the INSIDE tasks then all tasks become critical.

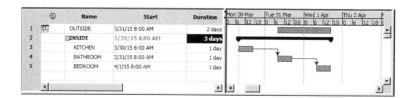

10. Updating Progress

As your project progresses you should track the work that has been completed. There are several methods that you can use to track work and update your project. The simplest method is to specify a completion percentage for each task. Each task has a "Percent Complete" field in the Update Task dialog shown below.

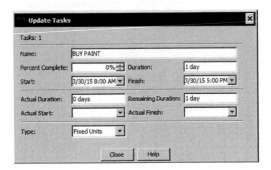

As you increase the completion percentage the Gantt chart will show a black bar to represent the work completed.

After you update tasks the Remaining, Actual and Percent Complete fields will also update throughout the project and the reports.

Another way to update tasks is to right-click on the column headings in the task spreadsheet and use the "Insert Column..." command to add the Percent Complete column to the spreadsheet.

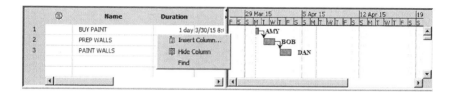

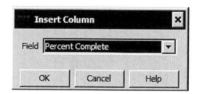

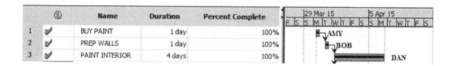

The Percent Complete information can quickly be changed by directly editing the task spreadsheet.

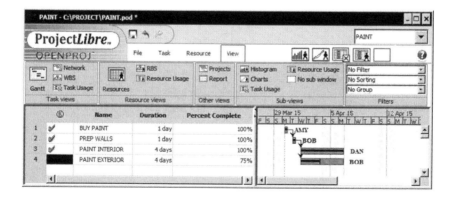

Another method of updating tasks is to enter the Actual Start and Actual Finish dates. When you create a task the software automatically creates baseline Start and Finish dates, but it also automatically creates the Actual Start and Actual Finish dates. Using the Percent Complete field updates these actual dates, however, you may also enter that data directly into those fields.

The Update Tasks dialog is shown below. You may enter the date with the format "m/d/yy h:mm AM" or you can click on the dropdown button to select a date from the calendar with the default starting or ending hours. As you adjust the fields in the dialog box, the other fields will update when you press the tab key or click on a different field. For example, if you change the Percent Complete and move to the next field the Actual Start and Actual Finish dates will change to show the new information.

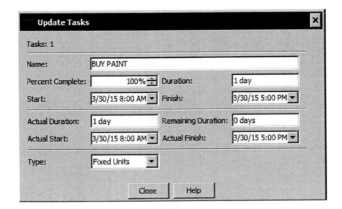

Yet another method to update the project is by selecting Update in the Project command group. The update project dialog shown below allows you to update the entire project through a specific date, or update the selected tasks through that date.

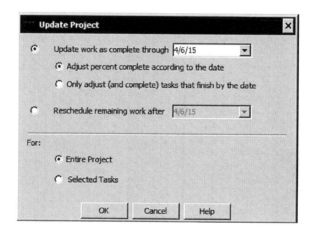

The Update Project dialog also allows you to reschedule uncompleted work after a specific date. This can be done for the entire project or only for the tasks you select

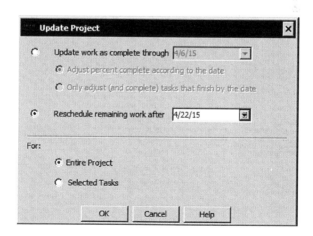

11. Sample Project

This chapter will use a kitchen remodel to show you how to use ProjectLibre to create and update a project plan.

11.1 Create Plan

After thinking about how you want your kitchen to look and doing some research you start your project. Using a spreadsheet, you may start with an estimate that looks similar to the table below.

TASKS	RESOURCE	HOURS	COST
PAYMENT #1	OWNER		
SITE PLANNING	MANAGER	4	$320
SITE PREP	OWNER	16	$0
ORDER MATERIALS	MANAGER	4	$320
PAYMENT #2	OWNER		
ELECTRICAL	ELECTRICIAN	8	$640
PLUMBING	PLUMBER	8	$640
DRYWALL	BUILDER	8	$640
PAINTING	PAINTER	8	$640
INSTALLATION	BUILDER		
INSTALL CABINETS	BUILDER	4	$320
INSTALL COUNTERTOPS	BUILDER	2	$160
INSTALL FLOORING	BUILDER	4	$320
INSTALL FIXTURES	BUILDER	4	$320
INSTALL APPLIANCES	BUILDER	2	$160
TOUCH UP	BUILDER	4	$320
FINAL INSPECTION	OWNER	4	$320
PAYMENT #3	OWNER		

MATERIALS		
	CABINETS	$2,000
	COUNTERTOPS	$2,000
	FLOORING	$2,000
	FIXTURES	$1,000
	APPLIANCES	$4,000
	KITCHEN REMODEL ESTIMATE	$16,120

Start a new project and name it KITCHEN REMODEL. Set the start date to May 5, 2017.

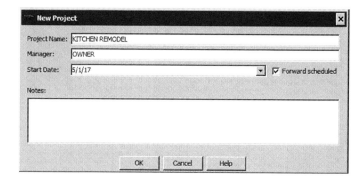

11.2 Create Calendar

Click on the File menu tab and then click on Calendar in the Project command group.

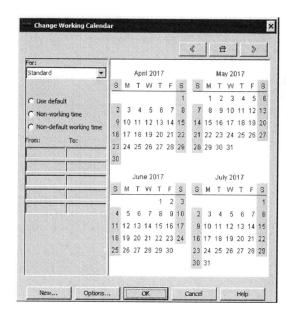

Click on the New button and create a new calendar named KITCHEN.

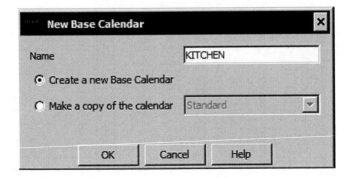

In this example you know the builder cannot work on the 8ᵗʰ or 29ᵗʰ of May. Hold the Ctrl key down and click on each of those dates, then select Non-working time and click OK.

In the Project Information dialog box set the Base Calendar to KITCHEN.

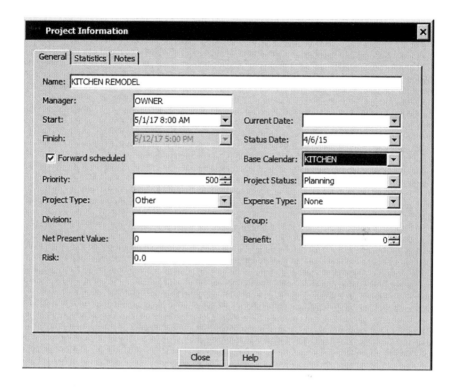

11.3 Create Tasks

Enter all the project tasks in the task spreadsheet.

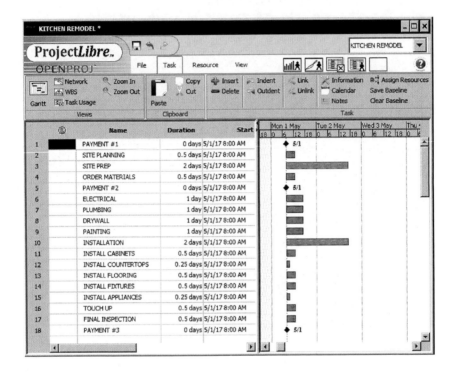

Hold the Ctrl key down and click on each of the installation subtasks. When they are all selected click on the Indent button in the Task command group to indent the installation tasks.

10	⊟ INSTALLATION	0.5 days	5/1/17 8:00 AM
11	INSTALL CABINETS	0.5 days	5/1/17 8:00 AM
12	INSTALL COUNTERTOPS	0.25 days	5/1/17 8:00 AM
13	INSTALL FLOORING	0.5 days	5/1/17 8:00 AM
14	INSTALL FIXTURES	0.5 days	5/1/17 8:00 AM
15	INSTALL APPLIANCES	0.25 days	5/1/17 8:00 AM

11.4 Link Tasks

Use the Predecessors column to link each task. In this example each task is simply linked to the task before it.

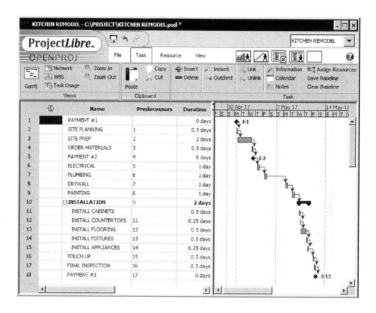

Note that it is possible to also link tasks by dragging in the bar chart. Use the mouse to drag one task to connect it to another to link them. A line and a small link icon will appear as you drag each task. Also, you may highlight two tasks and use the Link command button to link them.

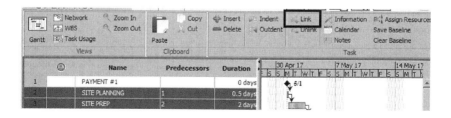

11.5 Create Resources

Enter the resources in the resource spreadsheet as shown below.

Name	Type	Standard Rate	Cost Per Use
BUILDER	Work	$70 / hour	$0
ELECTRICIAN	Work	$80 / hour	$0
MANAGER	Work	$60 / hour	$0
OWNER	Work	$0 / hour	$0
PAINTER	Work	$50 / hour	$0
PLUMBER	Work	$90 / hour	$0
CABINETS	Material	$0	$2,000
COUNTERTOPS	Material	$0	$2,000
FLOORING	Material	$0	$2,000
FIXTURES	Material	$0	$1,000
APPLIANCES	Material	$0	$4,000

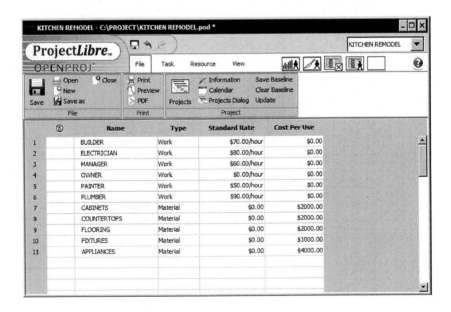

11.6 Assign Resources

Double click on the PAYMENT #1 task to open the Task Information dialog. Click on the Resources tab and click on the button at the right to assign resources.

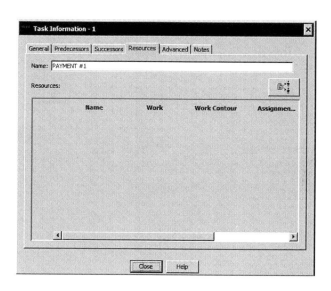

Select OWNER and click Assign and then close both dialogs.

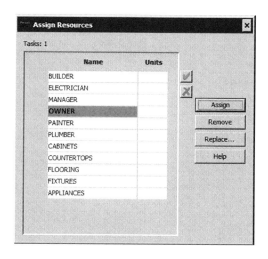

To Assign multiple tasks to the same resource at one time use the Ctrl key and the mouse to select the tasks. Then click on the Assign Resources button in the Task command group and click the Assign button. The Assign Resources button may also be used for a single task.

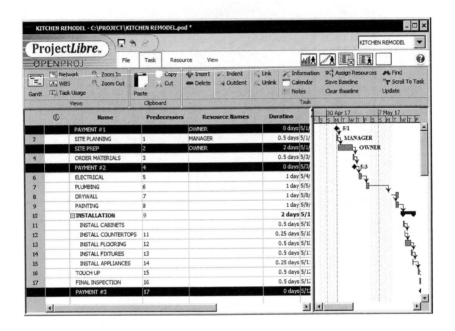

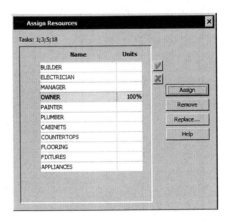

• MANAGING PROJECTLIBRE •

Continue adding all the resources until your task spreadsheet looks like the screen shown below.

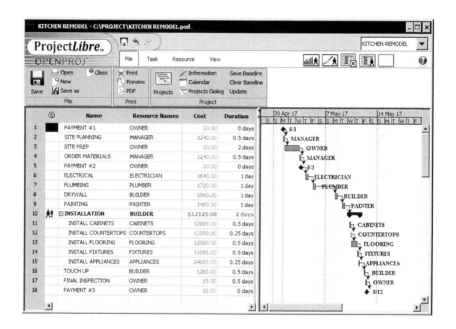

Note that the material resources have been added to the INSTALL tasks and BUILDER has been added to INSTALLATION causing an error. The standard method is to add both the material and work to each task.

10	♣!	⊟ **INSTALLATION**	**BUILDER**	$12120.00	2 days
11		INSTALL CABINETS	CABINETS	$2000.00	0.5 days
12		INSTALL COUNTERTOPS	COUNTERTOPS	$2000.00	0.25 days
13		INSTALL FLOORING	FLOORING	$2000.00	0.5 days
14		INSTALL FIXTURES	FIXTURES	$1000.00	0.5 days
15		INSTALL APPLIANCES	APPLIANCES	$4000.00	0.25 days

10	⊟ **INSTALLATION**		$12120.00	2 days
11	INSTALL CABINETS	CABINETS;BUILDER	$2280.00	0.5 days
12	INSTALL COUNTERTOPS	COUNTERTOPS;BU...	$2140.00	0.25 days
13	INSTALL FLOORING	FLOORING;BUILDER	$2280.00	0.5 days
14	INSTALL FIXTURES	FIXTURES;BUILDER	$1280.00	0.5 days
15	INSTALL APPLIANCES	APPLIANCES;BUIL...	$4140.00	0.25 days

11.7 Review Baseline

Once the information has been entered into the project it is a good time to review and set a baseline. The original estimate, without knowing detailed rates, was $16,120. In the Project Details report we can see that our new estimate is $15,200.

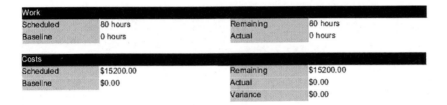

Work			
Scheduled	80 hours	Remaining	80 hours
Baseline	0 hours	Actual	0 hours

Costs			
Scheduled	$15200.00	Remaining	$15200.00
Baseline	$0.00	Actual	$0.00
		Variance	$0.00

You should also review the resource usage information and the resource histogram to make sure that resources are not overbooked.

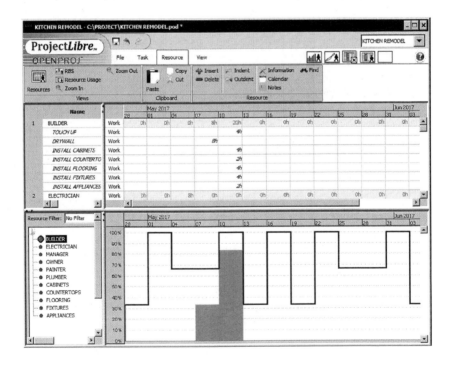

The resources are not overbooked and the expected time and budget seems close to our original estimate so now is a good time to save the baseline and print the reports.

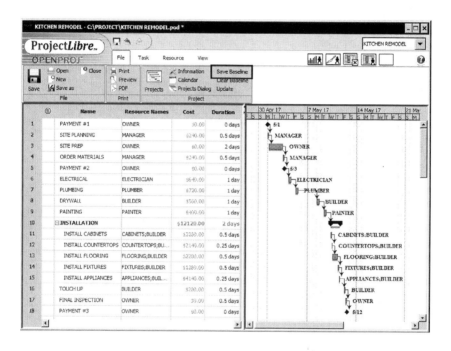

Resource ID	Resource						
1	BUILDER						
Task ID	Task	Work	Assignment Units	Assignment		Start	Finish
16	TOUCH UP	4 hours	100%	0 days		5/12/17 8:00 AM	5/12/17 1:00 PM
8	DRYWALL	8 hours	100%	0 days		5/8/17 8:00 AM	5/8/17 5:00 PM
11	INSTALL CABINETS	4 hours	100%	0 days		5/10/17 8:00 AM	5/10/17 1:00 PM
12	INSTALL COUNTERTOPS	2 hours	100%	0 days		5/10/17 1:00 PM	5/10/17 3:00 PM
13	INSTALL FLOORING	4 hours	100%	0 days		5/10/17 3:00 PM	5/11/17 10:00 AM
14	INSTALL FIXTURES	4 hours	100%	0 days		5/11/17 10:00 AM	5/11/17 3:00 PM
15	INSTALL APPLIANCES	2 hours	100%	0 days		5/11/17 3:00 PM	5/11/17 5:00 PM
		28 hours					
2	ELECTRICIAN						
Task ID	Task	Work	Assignment Units	Assignment		Start	Finish
6	ELECTRICAL	8 hours	100%	0 days		5/4/17 8:00 AM	5/4/17 5:00 PM
		8 hours					
3	MANAGER						
Task ID	Task	Work	Assignment Units	Assignment		Start	Finish
2	SITE PLANNING	4 hours	100%	0 days		5/1/17 8:00 AM	5/1/17 1:00 PM
4	ORDER MATERIALS	4 hours	100%	0 days		5/3/17 1:00 PM	5/3/17 5:00 PM
		8 hours					
4	OWNER						
Task ID	Task	Work	Assignment Units	Assignment		Start	Finish
1	PAYMENT #1	0 hours	100%	0 days		5/1/17 8:00 AM	5/1/17 8:00 AM

11.8 Update Progress

Currently the project is scheduled to start on May 1st and end on May 12th. However, assume that there has been a delay and the project must start on May 3rd. Click on the Update button in the Project command group to reschedule the project.

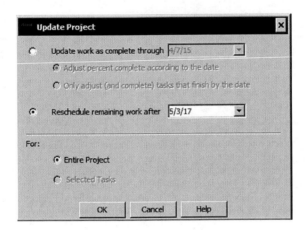

The project has a new completion date of May 18th.

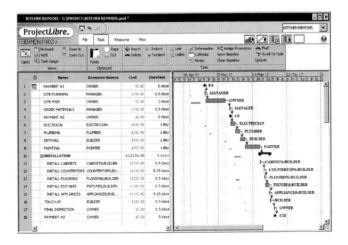

Update each task in the project up to the TOUCH UP task. You may use the Update Project dialog and update work through a date or update each task individually. Many find it convenient to add the Percent Complete column to the task spreadsheet as shown below.

	ⓘ	Name	Resource Names	Baseline Cost	Cost	Percent Complete	Duration
1	🖫 ✔	PAYMENT #1	OWNER	$0.00	$0.00	100%	0 days
2	✔	SITE PLANNING	MANAGER	$240.00	$240.00	100%	0.5 days
3	✔	SITE PREP	OWNER	$0.00	$0.00	100%	2 days
4	✔	ORDER MATERIALS	MANAGER	$240.00	$240.00	100%	0.5 days
5	✔	PAYMENT #2	OWNER	$0.00	$0.00	100%	0 days
6	✔	ELECTRICAL	ELECTRICIAN	$640.00	$640.00	100%	1 day
7	✔	PLUMBING	PLUMBER	$720.00	$720.00	100%	1 day
8	✔	DRYWALL	BUILDER	$560.00	$560.00	100%	1 day
9	✔	PAINTING	PAINTER	$400.00	$400.00	100%	1 day
10	✔	☐ INSTALLATION		$12120.00	$12120.00	100%	2 days
11	✔	INSTALL CABINETS	CABINETS;BUILDER	$2280.00	$2280.00	100%	0.5 days
12	✔	INSTALL COUNTERTOPS	COUNTERTOPS;BUILDER	$2140.00	$2140.00	100%	0.25 days
13	✔	INSTALL FLOORING	FLOORING;BUILDER	$2280.00	$2280.00	100%	0.5 days
14	✔	INSTALL FIXTURES	FIXTURES;BUILDER	$1280.00	$1280.00	100%	0.5 days
15	✔	INSTALL APPLIANCES	APPLIANCES;BUILDER	$4140.00	$4140.00	100%	0.25 days
16		TOUCH UP	BUILDER	$280.00	$1120.00	0%	2 days
17		FINAL INSPECTION	OWNER	$0.00	$0.00	0%	0.5 days
18		PAYMENT #3	OWNER	$0.00	$0.00	0%	0 days

Now change the duration of the TOUCH UP task from 4 hours to 16 hours, which is two days. These types of small adjustments can often occur. As you can see below the Baseline Cost has increased from $280 to $1,120 to reflect the additional time the BUILDER must spend on the TOUCH UP task.

Baseline Cost	Cost	Percent Complete	Duration
$280.00	$1120.00	0%	2 days

Update the remaining tasks to be completed and your project should look similar to the screen below.

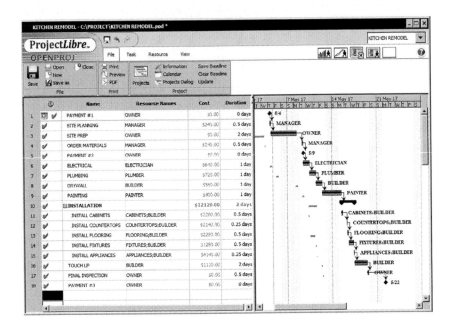

The Project Details report should show that the Baseline finish moved from 5/12/17 to 5/22/17 and the expected cost of $15,200 ended up at an actual cost of $16,040.

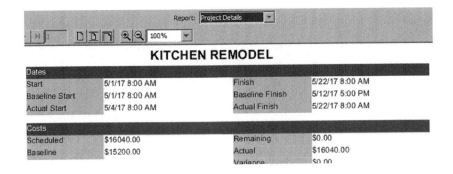

11.9 Close Project

The closing phase involves releasing the final deliverables to the customer, handing over project documentation, terminating supplier contracts, releasing project resources and communicating project closure to all stakeholders. The final step is to undertake an evaluation to determine the extent to which the project was successful and note any lessons learned for future projects.

Once you've completed the project, it's likely that you will no longer need immediate access to the files, and you may want to archive them. This may include making a copy of the project files and some hard copies of the reports and other items. You may want to print the reports to PDF files so they can also be saved electronically as well.

Finally, no matter how small or large a project is, find a way to celebrate a successful project. Take time to recognize the team members and all the stakeholders that took part in the project. Appreciation is a fundamental human need. Effective project managers understand the psychology of praising others for their good work and encourage others to initiate it in their working relationships.

12. Glossary

Acceptance – The act of approving the deliverables.

Activity – A task needed to complete the work.

Actual Cost (AC) – The actual cost of the work performed.

Assumptions – Beliefs considered to be true for planning.

Bar Chart – A chart where horizontal bars represent lengths of times for scheduled activities.

Baseline – The original scope, cost or schedule.

Benefit Analysis – Determining the costs and benefits.

Bill of Materials (BOM) – A hierarchy of the materials needed to complete the project.

Brainstorming – Gathering ideas from participants.

Budget at completion (BAC) – The planned project budget.

Change Control System – A system to formally accept, review, and act upon project change requests.

Claim – A disagreement between the buyer and the seller.

Closing – The orderly conclusion of the project.

Configuration Management – A documented process of controlling the features of the product.

Constraint – Any influence on the project that may limit the options.

Contract – A binding agreement between two parties.

Control Chart – Used to show project performance over time.

Cost Budgeting – A process of assigning a cost to an individual work package.

Cost Estimating – The process of calculating the costs, by category, of the identified resources to complete the project work.

Cost Performance Index (CPI) – An index that measures how well the project is performing on cost: CPI = EV/AC.

Cost Variance (CV) – The difference between the earned value (EV) and the actual cost (AC).

Critical Path Method (CPM) – A process of using a time path to reveal which activities are considered critical to the project.

Crashing – This is the addition of more resources to activities on the critical path in order to complete the project earlier.

Decision Tree Analysis – A type of analysis that determines which of two decisions is the best.

Deliverable – A product or service created from a project.

Direct Costs – A direct project expense.

Dummy Activity – An activity with no duration used show relationships in the project diagram.

Earned value (EV) – The value of the work that has been completed and the budget for that work, the equation for which is EV = %Complete × BAC.

Estimate at Completion (EAC) – A hypothesis of what the total cost of the project will be.

Estimate to complete (ETC) – Represents how much more money is needed to complete the project work. Its formula is ETC = EAC – AC.

Evaluation Criteria – Used to rate and score proposals from sellers.

Fast Tracking – Doing activities in parallel that are normally done sequentially.

Feedback – A response, question for clarification, or other confirmation once a sent message is received.

Finish No Later Than (FNLT) – This constraint requires the project or activity to finish by a predetermined date.

Finish-to-Finish – This relationship means Task A must complete before Task B can complete.

Finish-to-Start – This relationship means Task A must complete before Task B can begin. This is the most common relationship.

Float – The amount of time a task can be delayed without delaying project completion.

Force Majeure – A powerful and unexpected event, such as a hurricane or other disaster.

Fragnets – Portions of a network diagram that branch off the project and are not on the critical path.

Future Value – A formula to calculate the future value of present money.

Gantt Chart – A chart where horizontal bars represent lengths of times for scheduled activities.

Indirect Cost – Costs that are not direct project expenses like rent.

Initiating – This process group begins the project.

Invitation for Bid – A document from the buyer to the seller.

ISO 9000 – A method of following procedures created by an organization.

Lag – Time added to a task to move it away from the project start.

Lead – Time subtracted from a task to bring it closer to the project start date.

Lessons Learned – Things the project manager and project team have learned throughout the project.

Metrics – Measurements of the performance of a project.

Mitigation – Reduction of the probability or impact of a risk.

Network Diagram – A flow chart that includes all the project elements and how they relate.

Planned value (PV) – The worth of the work that should be completed by a specific time in the project schedule.

Precedence Diagramming Method (PDM) – A method that diagrams activities in boxes, called nodes, and connects the boxes with arrows.

Present Value – A formula to calculate the present value of future money.

Process Groups – The five project stages of initiation, planning, executing, controlling and closing.

Project Scope – The deliverables the project is creating.

Program Evaluation and Review Technique (PERT) – A scheduling tool that uses a weighted average formula to predict the length of activities and the project.

Project – A temporary endeavor undertaken to create a product or service.

Project Charter – The charter authorizes the project, the project manager, and the required resources to complete the project work.

Project Life Cycle – The duration of the project, composed of all the individual project phases within the project.

Project Manager – The individual accountable for all aspects of a project.

Project Phase – A manageable subsection of a project.

Project Slack – The total time the project can be delayed without passing expected completion date.

Quality Assurance – A process in which overall performance is evaluated to ensure the project meets the quality standards.

Quotation – A document from the seller to the buyer used to determine price.

Resources – People, equipment, material and other costs needed to perform the tasks in a project.

Resource Leveling – A technique in which start and finish dates are adjusted based on resource constraints with the goal of balancing demand for resources with the available supply.

Resource Breakdown Structure (RBS) – A project view that organizes and displays resources in groups.

Return on Investment (ROI) – The project's financial return in proportion to the amount of monies invested in the project.

Risk – An unplanned event that can have a positive or negative influence on the project success.

Schedule Variance – The difference between the planned work and the earned work.

Scope creep – Uncontrolled changes or continuous growth in a project's scope.

Sensitivity Analysis – This examines each project risk on its own merit to assess the impact on the project.

Sole Source – When only one qualified seller that exists for a resource.

Stakeholders – The individuals, groups, and communities that have a vested interest in the outcome of a project.

Start No Earlier Than (SNET) – This constraint requires that the project or activity not start earlier than the predetermined date.

Start No Later Than (SNLT) – This constraint requires that the activity begin by a predetermined date.

Start-to-Finish – This relationship requires that Task A start so that Task B may finish; it is unusual and is rarely used.

Start-to-Start – This relationship means Task A must start before Task B can start. This relationship allows both activities to happen in tandem.

Statement of work (SOW) – This fully describes the work to be completed, the product to be supplied, or both.

Statistical Sampling – A process of choosing a percentage of results at random for inspection.

Subproject – Exists under a parent project but follows its own schedule to completion.

Three Point Estimate – An estimate that uses optimistic, most likely, and pessimistic values.

Top-Down Estimating – A project estimate based on the total of a similar project.

Variance – The difference between what was planned and what was experienced.

Variance at Completion (VAC) – The difference between the BAC and the EAC. Its formula is $VAC = BAC - EAC$.

Work breakdown structure (WBS) – A hierarchical chart with nodes that represent all the tasks in a project.

Workaround – An unplanned response to a risk that was not identified or accepted.

35006877R00057

Made in the USA
Lexington, KY
30 March 2019